A Mark Dahle Portfolio

Monkey Brains On Big Ocean

Little Gibbon's Big Adventures #2

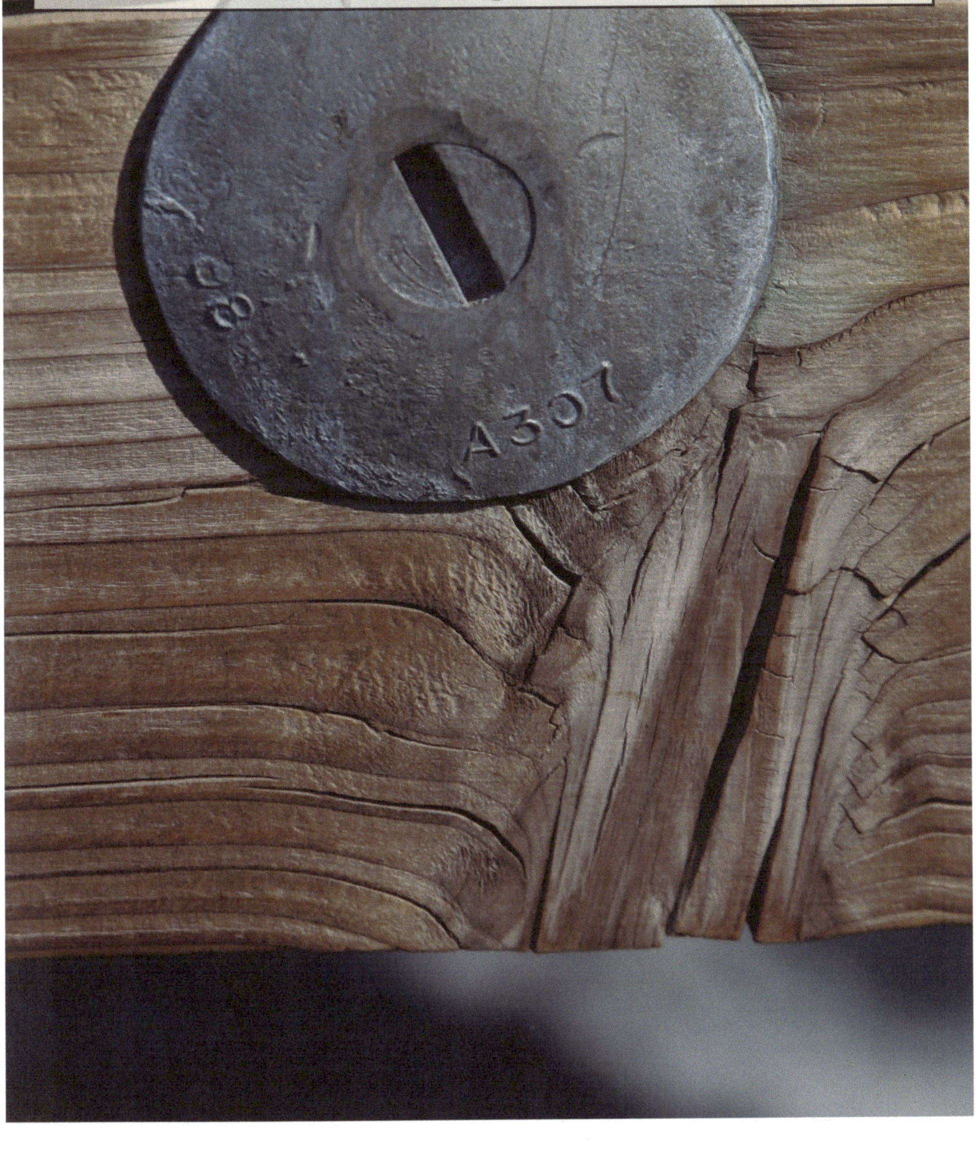

This is the second story about a gibbon who liked adventures. All the other gibbons called him Monkey Brains.

Books in this series include:
1. Monkey Brains On Big River
2. Monkey Brains On Big Ocean
3. Monkey Brains On Big Mountain
4. Monkey Brains In Big Desert

~ ~ ~

Mark Dahle Portfolios can be read in a few minutes and enjoyed for a lifetime.

Unlike many picture books, the text in this book is not related to the art. This might seem weird at first. One thing that makes it better is to order more portfolios until you get used to it. Fortunately, space is provided on the pages for you to draw your own pictures of Big Ocean if you like.

This portfolio includes a beautiful 36 x 24 inch painting (at the right), twenty-six great photos from Spokane, Washington, and a story about an adventurer who called himself Little Gibbon.

Photographs in this book are available in limited editions. See http://www.MarkDahle.com for more information and for previews of upcoming portfolios.

We do our best to create portfolios free of editing mistakes. But it's hard to catch everything. We reward people who report errors in any Mark Dahle portfolio. For details see MarkDahle.com/Typos.html or email MarkDahle@aol.com with the subject line "Typos." Thanks!

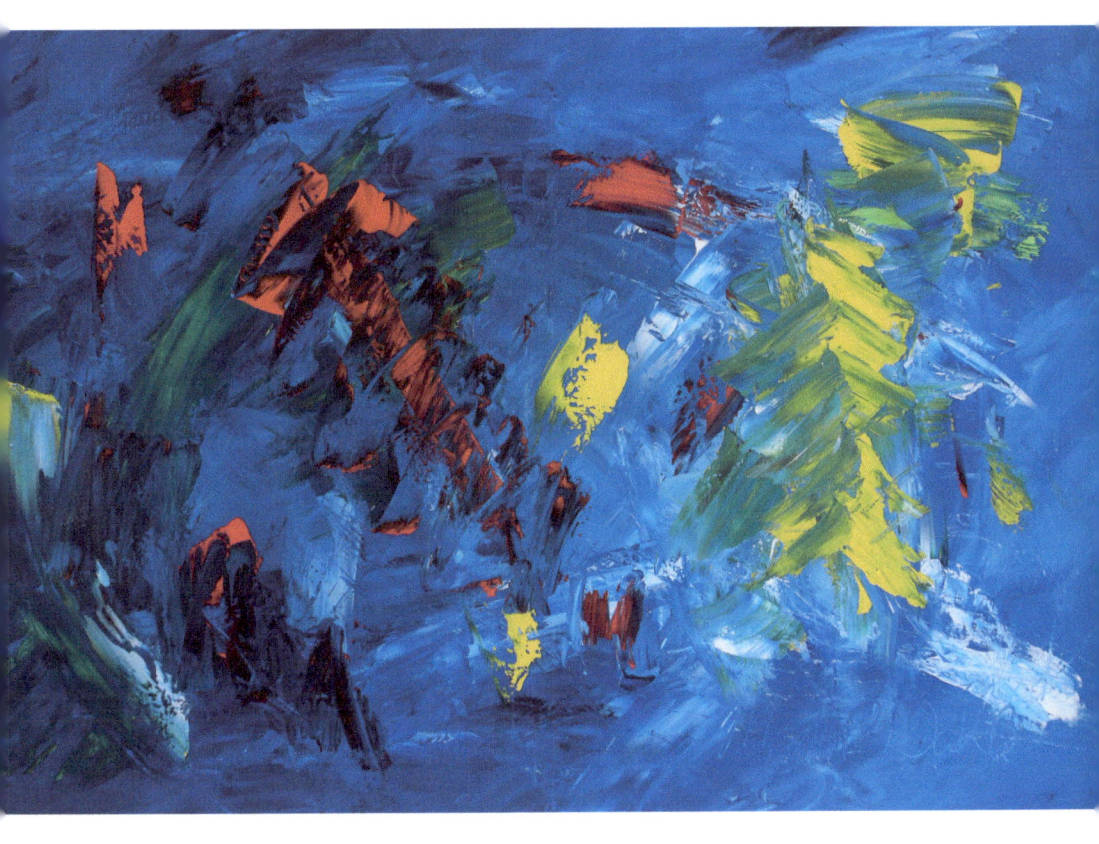

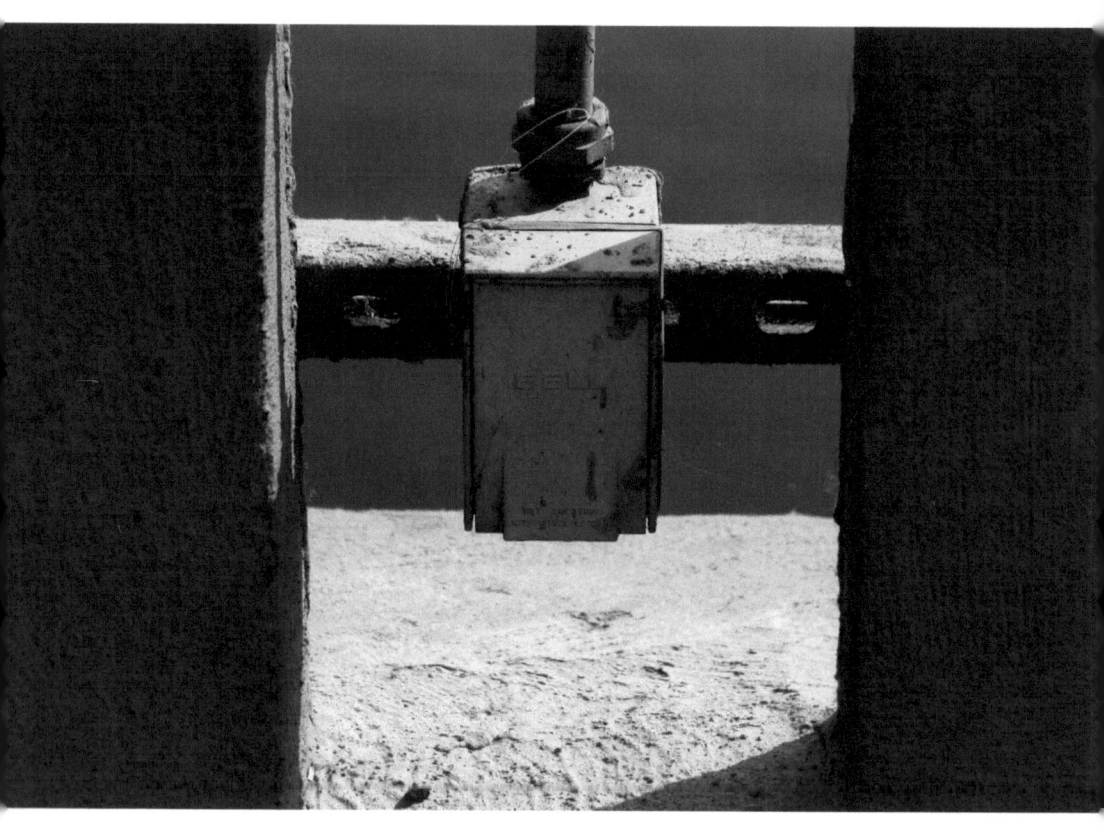

Gibbons usually like to swing from tree to tree. But the youngest gibbon in one family preferred adventures. He would swing in trees if it would get him to a new adventure. Otherwise he wasn't interested. As a result, all the gibbons he knew called him Monkey Brains. He called himself Little Gibbon, since he was still growing and learning lots.

One morning Little Gibbon was dreaming about having an adventure. He woke up when he stretched and scraped his knuckles against something hard.

What could that be? He opened his eyes.

He was not in his bed. At first he thought he was still dreaming. Everything was white except for what was up close. His hand had hit the side of a canoe. What was he doing in a canoe?

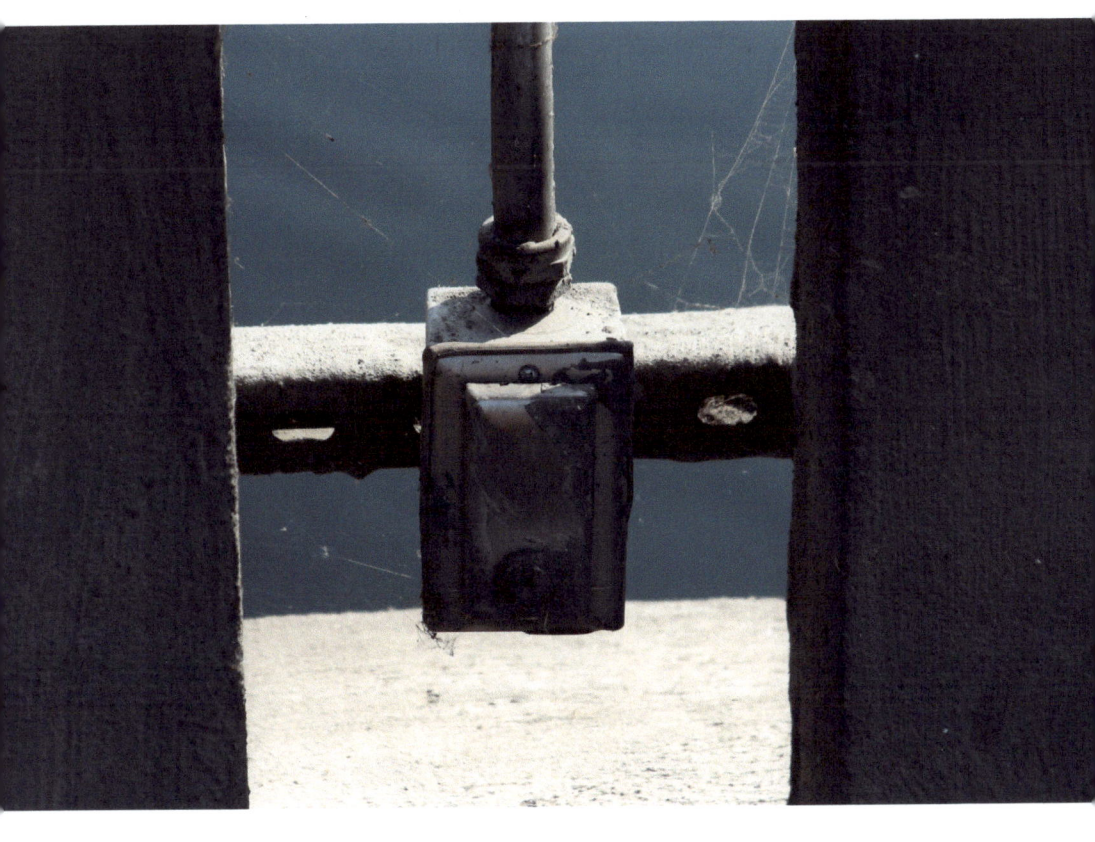

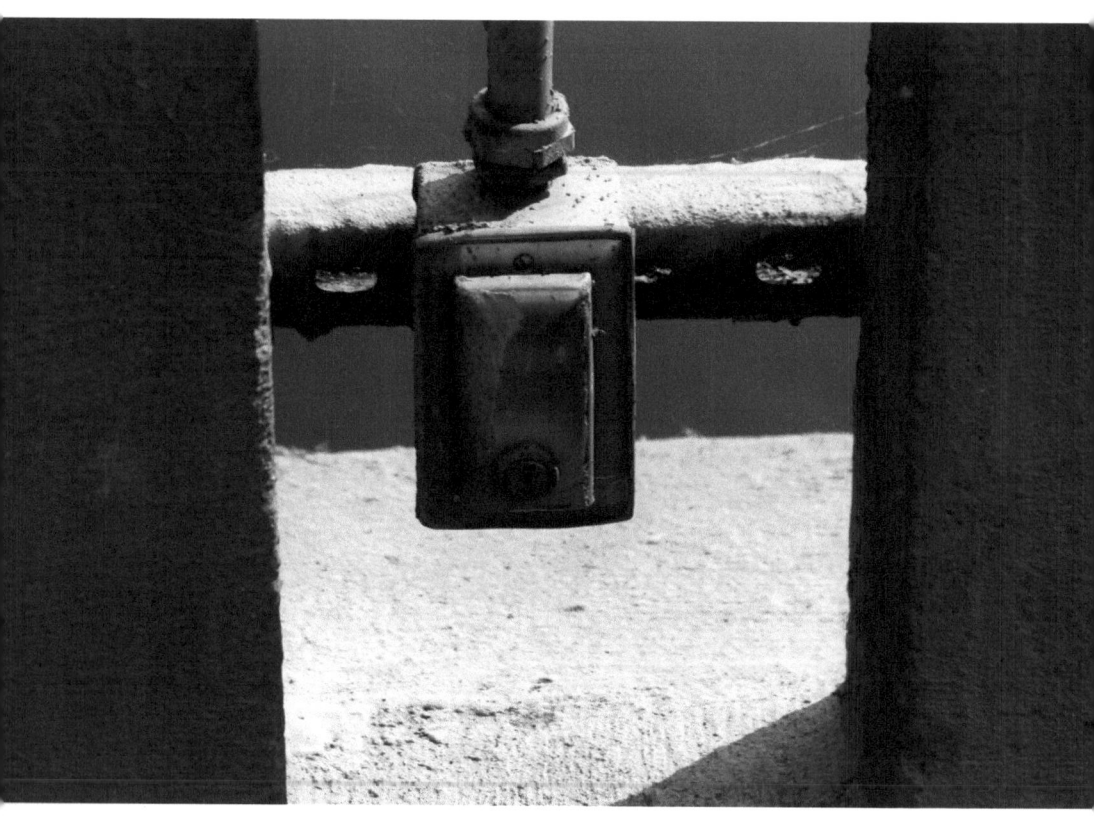

Then he remembered. He had fallen asleep in his canoe on Big River.

But this didn't seem like Big River. His canoe was gently going up and down – *way* up and *way* down – on long swells. Big River never behaved like that. He must have made it all the way to Big Ocean!

"Big Ocean!" Little Gibbon cried. "We're going to have an adventure!"

Big Ocean smiled.

She liked Little Gibbon, because when he was around you never could tell what would happen next. And she was glad Little Gibbon liked adventures, because he was about to get one, fast. He had drifted into the Fog-Covered Shipping Lanes.

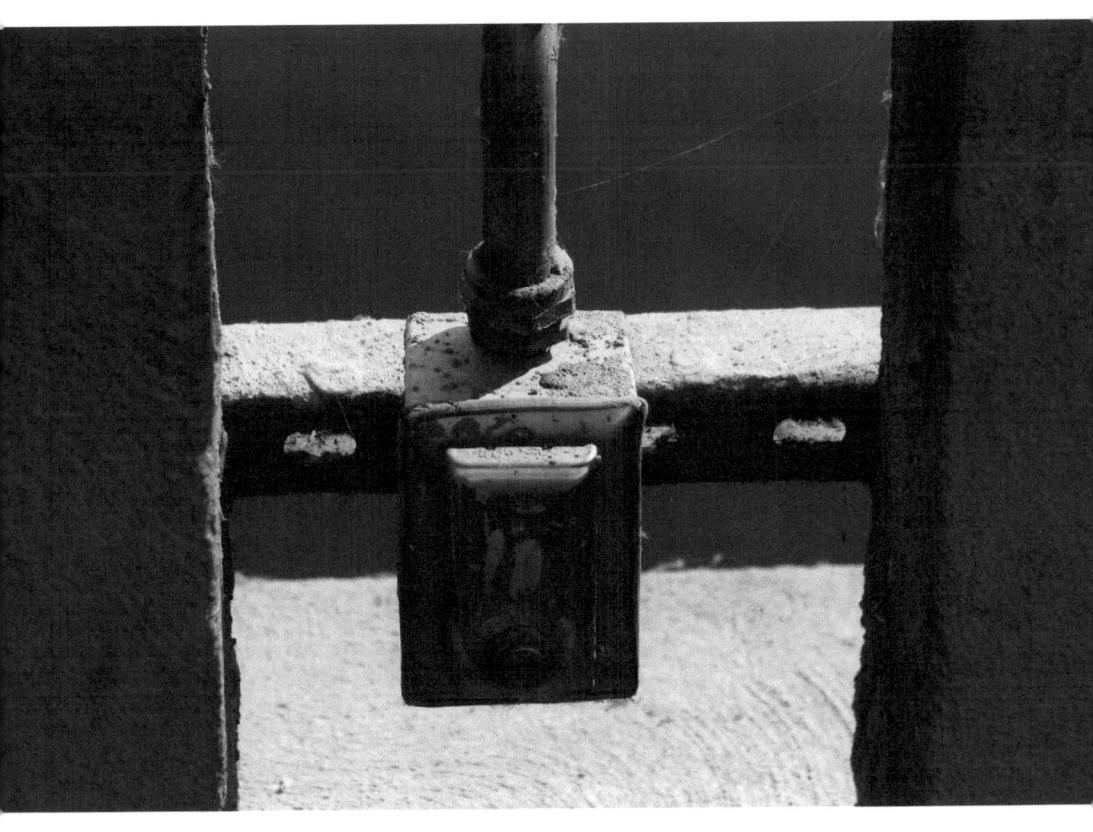

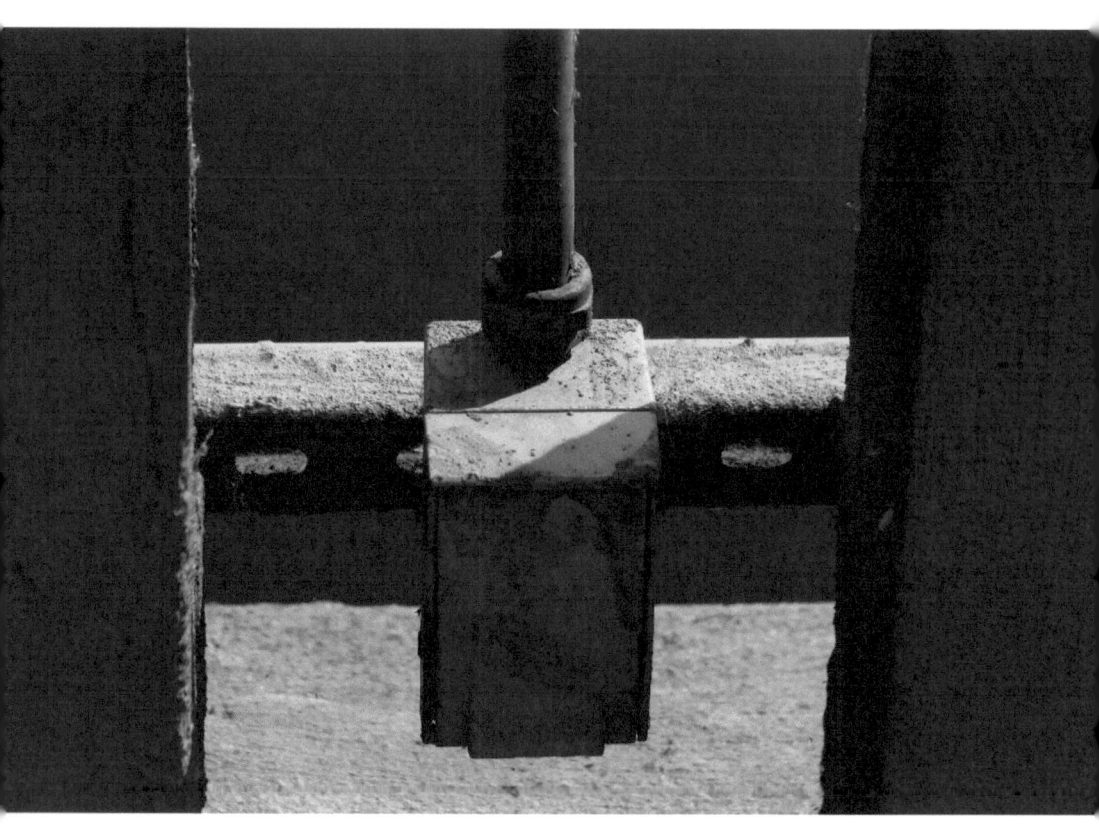

A horn sounded so close to Little Gibbon that he jumped, which caused his canoe to rock sideways in the swells. Little Gibbon got a little dizzy.

Little Gibbon couldn't see anything in the fog, but he could hear what sounded like an *immense* motor. Suddenly a tall cliff burst into view, jumping out of the fog. It was cutting through the water, with a wake on each side of it.

Little Gibbon looked up. Way up. He gasped. It was not a cliff. It was a ship. It was enormous, and it was coming straight towards him.

"Mooo – ooove," the ship's foghorn said.

Little Gibbon wished he had his paddle so he could. He wished he had his life preserver. He even wished (for just a moment) that he were safe in his bed at home.

Little Gibbon had no way to move the canoe out of the way. There was nothing to do but hang on to the canoe's sides and hope. He was in for an adventure!

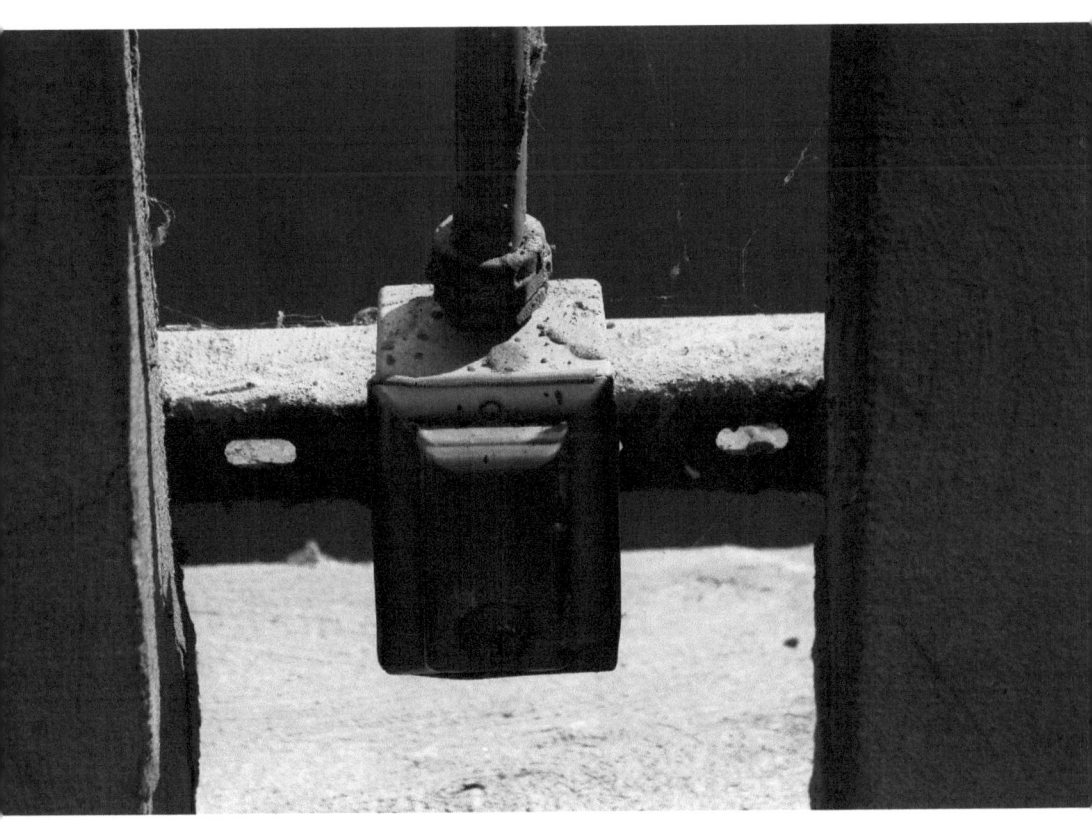

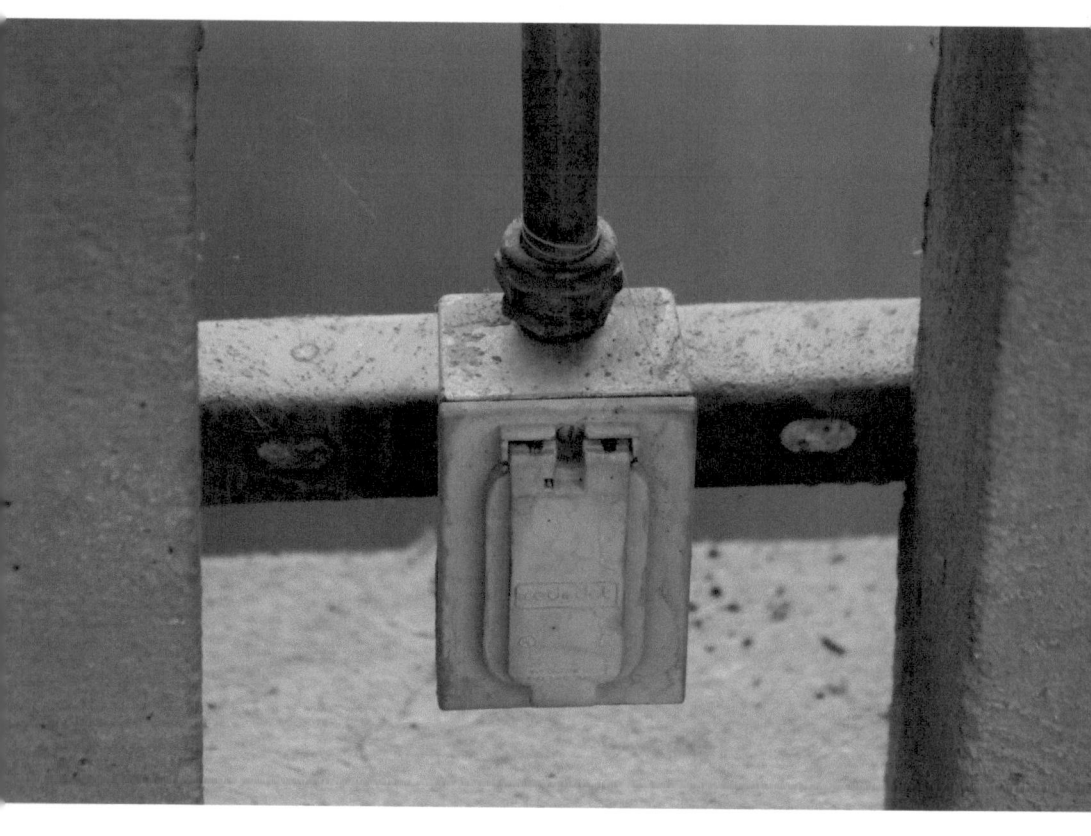

"Mooo – ooove," said the ship's foghorn, but not to Little Gibbon. The ship was too big to notice Little Gibbon. The ship came slicing through the water and just missed broadsiding the canoe. Little Gibbon's canoe bumped and scraped along the full length of the ship as it passed.

When Little Gibbon finally got to the end of the ship, the ship's wake sent Little Gibbon and his canoe tumbling down long foamy waves.

"Wheeee!" cried Little Gibbon. "Big Ocean! We're having an adventure!"

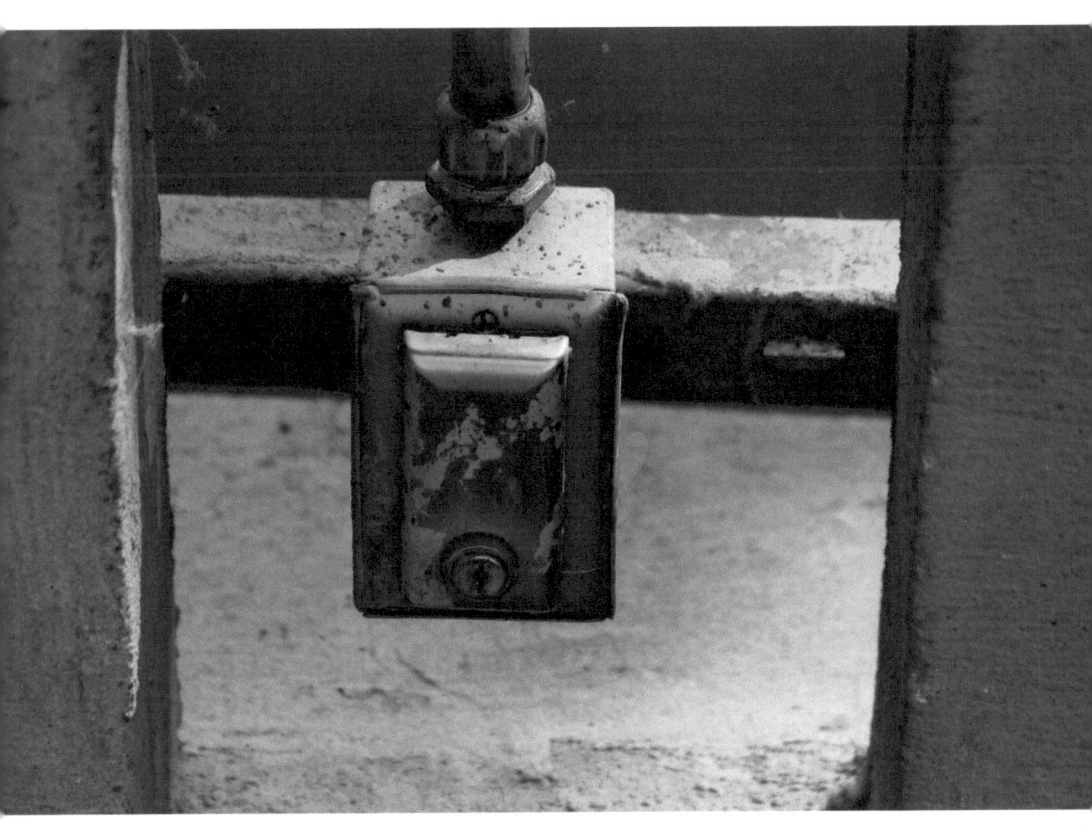

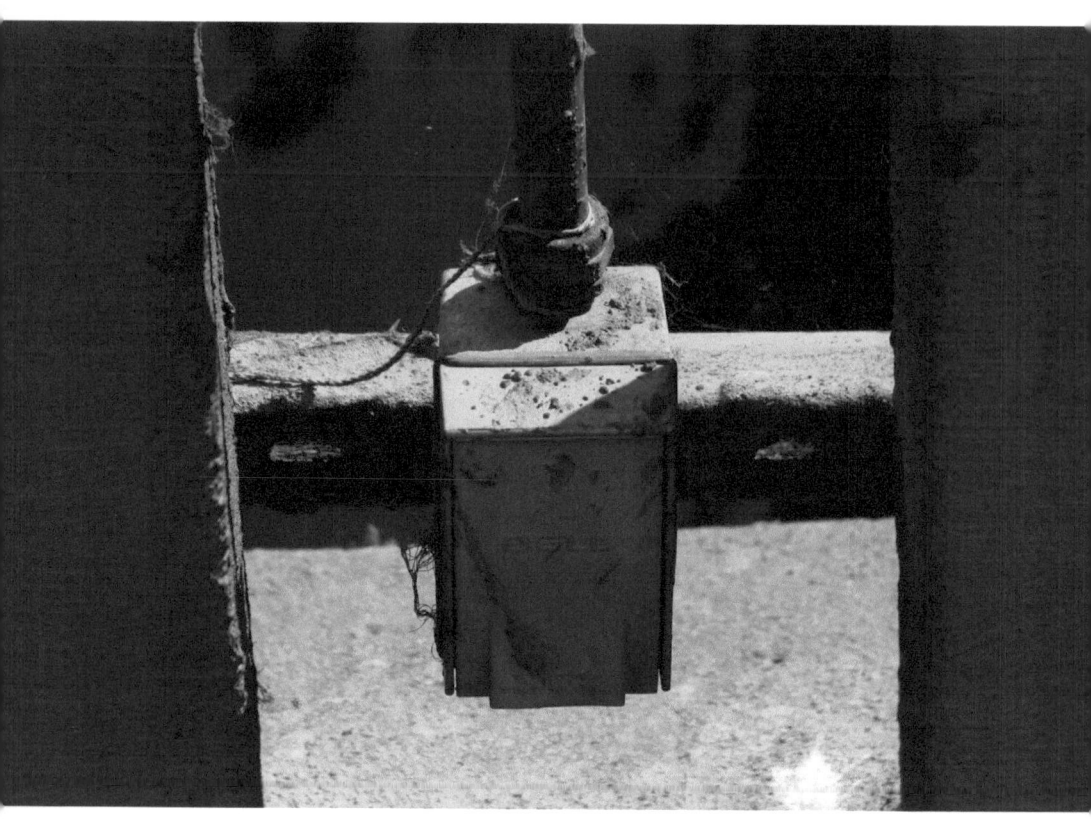

Big Ocean smiled.

Luckily for Little Gibbon, Big Ocean was in a good mood. A week ago, Big Ocean had been gray and gruff and had smashed against everything in her sight. But today Big Ocean was feeling peaceful. As a result, now that Little Gibbon was out of the Fog-Covered Shipping Lanes, there was very little danger unless he took a Giant Drink Of Saltwater.

Little Gibbon looked at Big Ocean and licked his lips. He was terribly thirsty. He had forgotten to bring any water. But he did have a cup.

"Big Ocean," Little Gibbon shouted, "I hope you don't mind, but I'm going to get a big drink of some of your water."

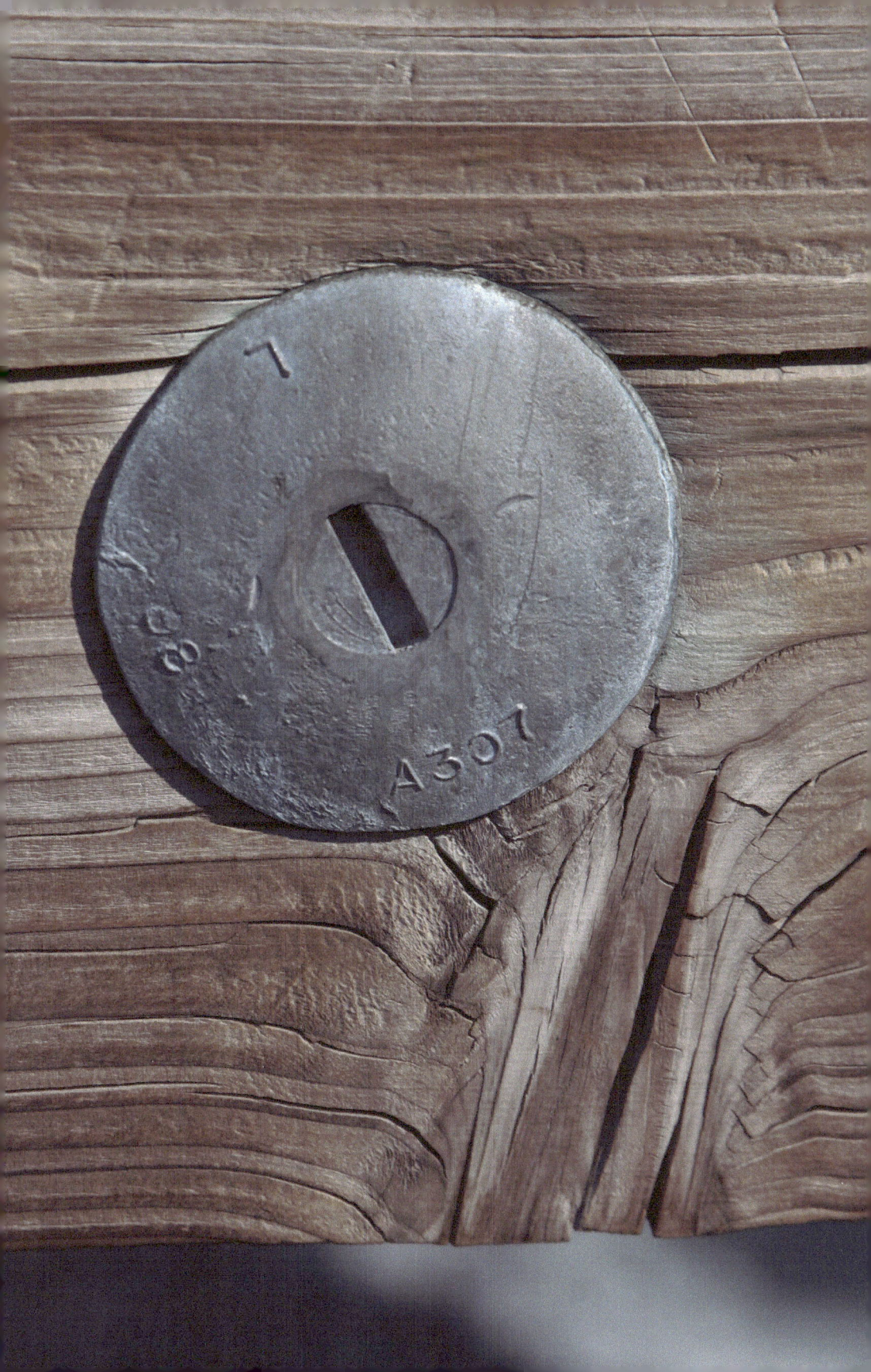

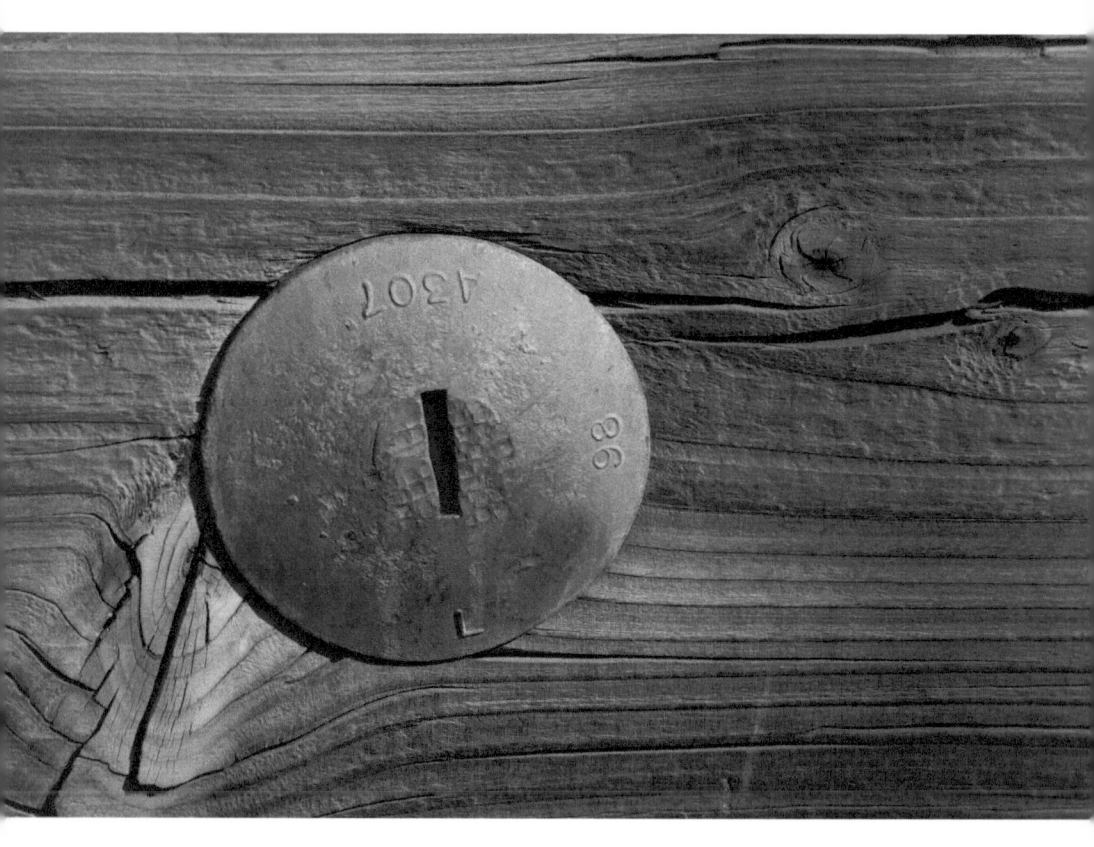

Big Ocean didn't mind. But the salt in Big Ocean made people thirsty. It never helped when anyone drank her water.

Little Gibbon filled his cup and licked his lips and was ready to take a big drink when a wave smacked his canoe. Most of the drink splashed into Little Gibbon's face instead of going down his throat.

"Oh, my eyes!" Little Gibbon cried. "They're burning!"

"Oh, my lips!" Little Gibbon cried. "They hurt where they're cracked!"

"Oh my throat!" Little Gibbon cried. "It's all dry and scratchy from the saltwater!"

Little Gibbon was glad he hadn't gotten a bigger drink.

But more than that? He was glad he was having an adventure.

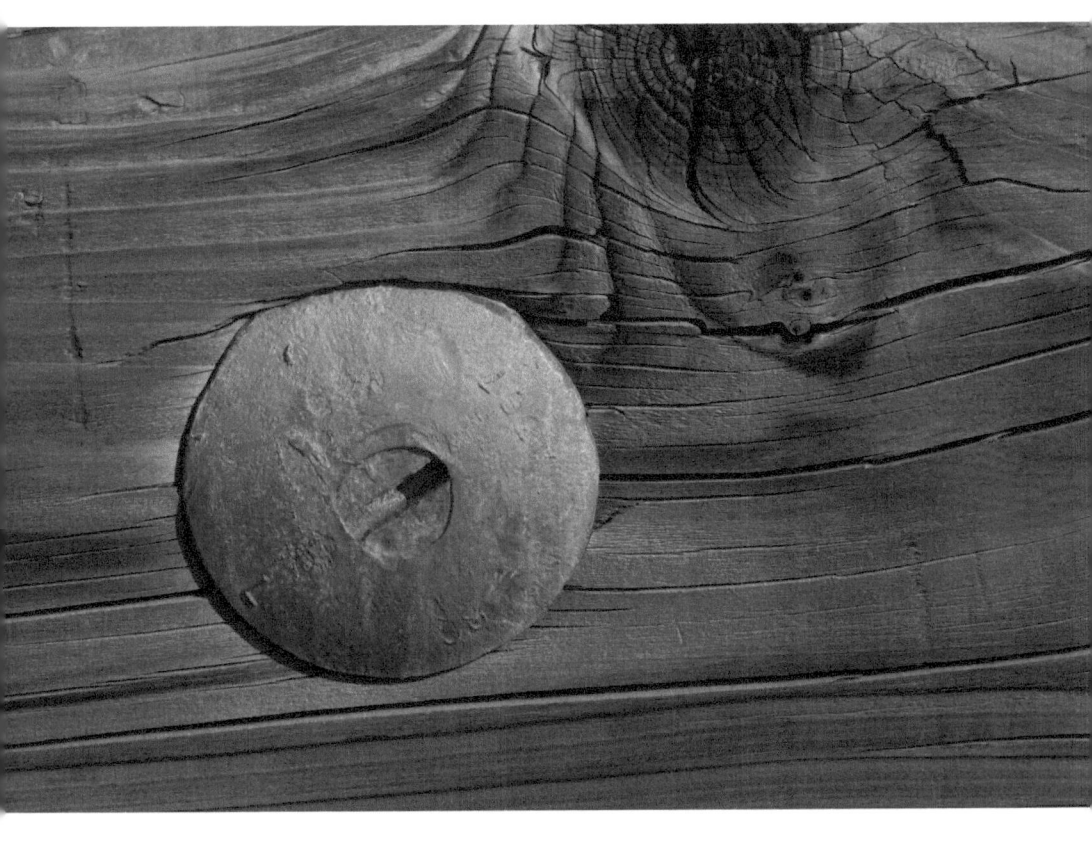

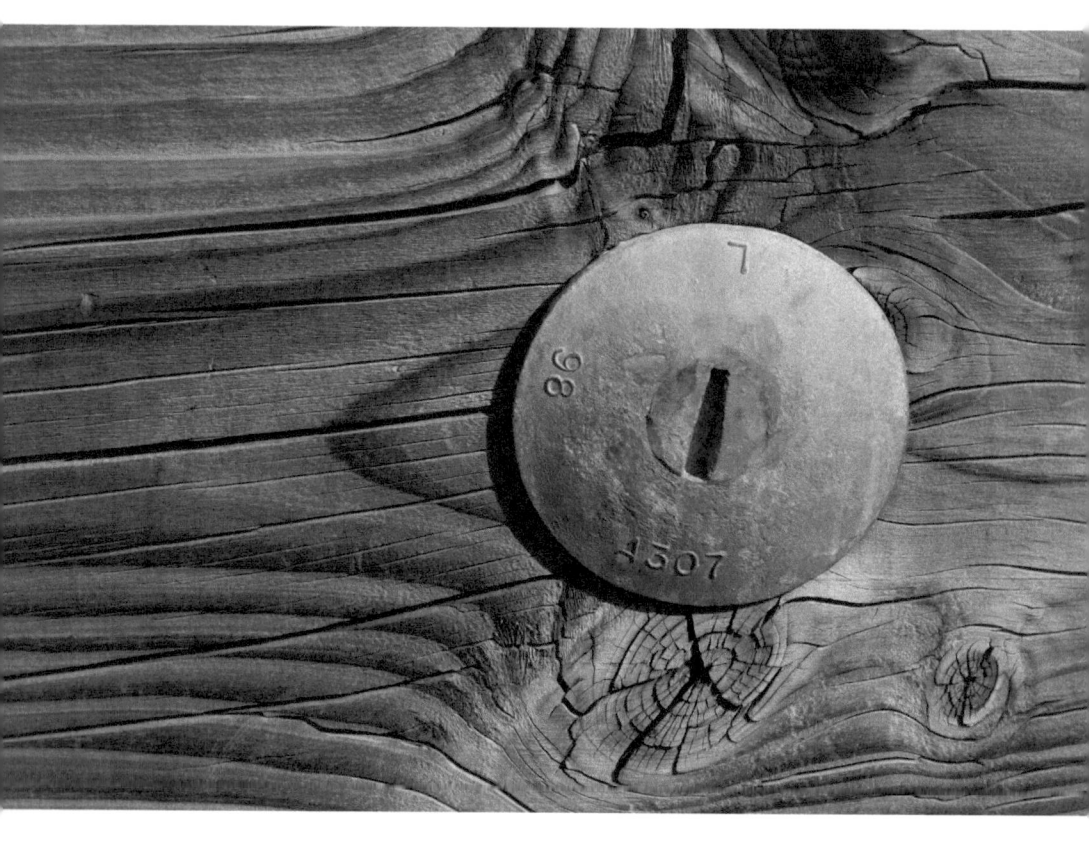

Big Ocean smiled. She was glad Little Gibbon had made it through the Fog-Covered Shipping Lanes and had mostly avoided taking a Giant Drink Of Saltwater. Now there was very little danger except for the Bay Of Sharks With Big Teeth.

Little Gibbon would be fine as long as he stayed completely inside his canoe.

Little Gibbon was dangling his hand in Big Ocean. The salt water stung where he had scrapped his knuckle against the side of the canoe. Little Gibbon looked down. He was bleeding a little, and the blood was leaving a trail in the water.

Several black triangles were racing towards the canoe.

Curious what they might be, Little Gibbon looked over the side into the water. He was staring into the open mouth of an approaching shark with very sharp teeth.

Little Gibbon yanked his hand out of the water. "Go away," shouted Little Gibbon. "There's nothing to eat here."

The shark wasn't so sure. His jaws snapped shut where Little Gibbon's hand had been. Luckily for Little Gibbon, the shark's jaws closed on nothing but water and air.

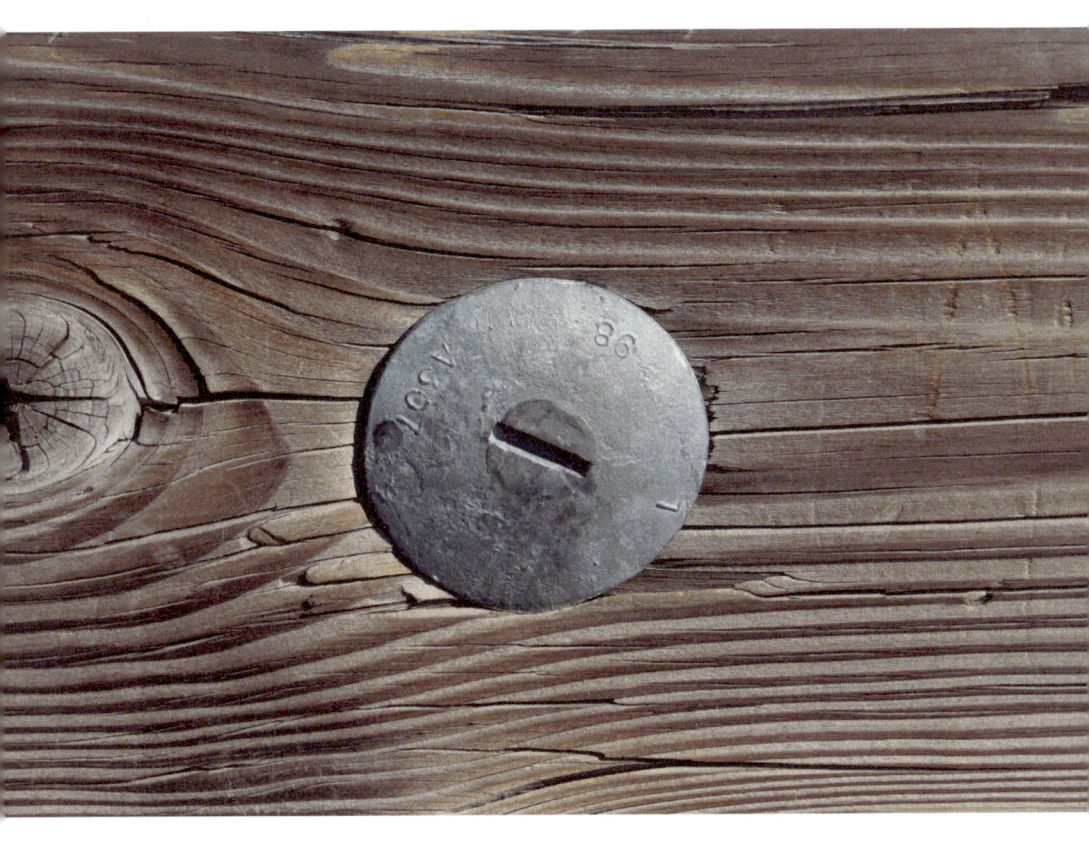

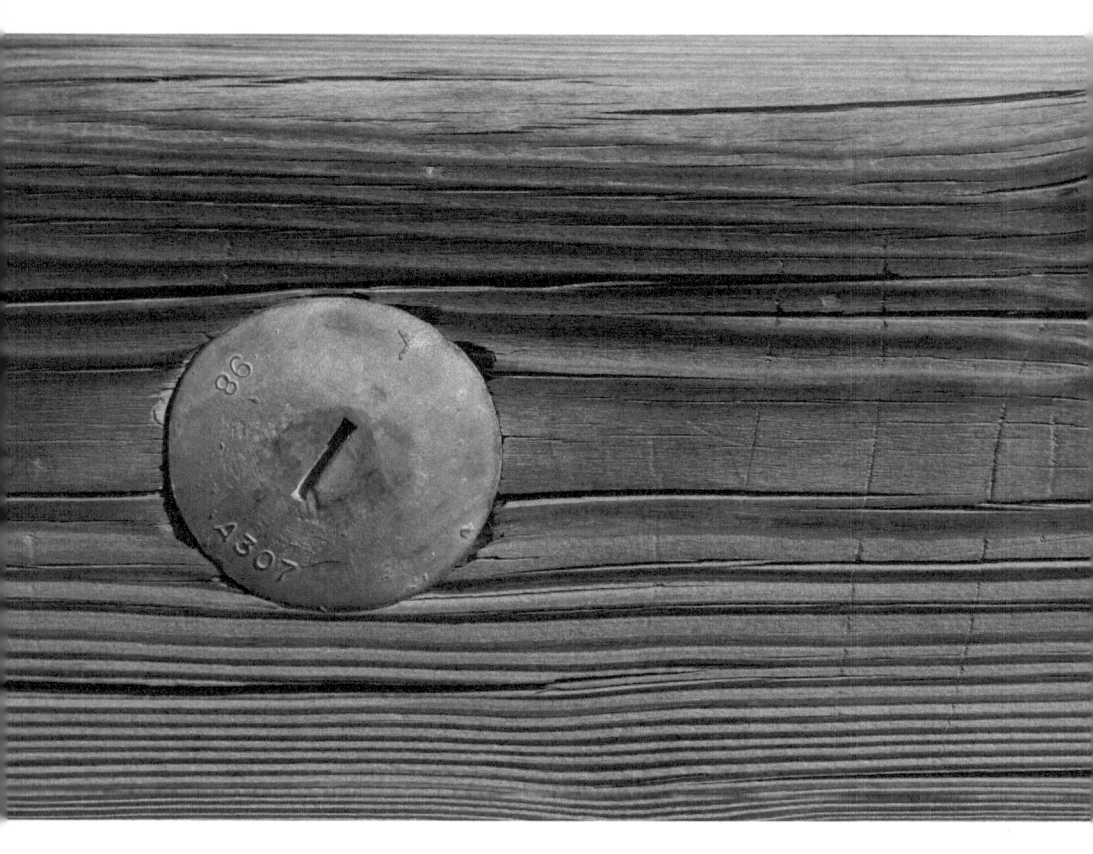

One or two more sharks came by and bumped the canoe, testing to see whether the canoe itself might be tasty.

"Big Ocean," Little Gibbon cried, "this is almost *too much* of an adventure!"

Luckily, within a few minutes Little Gibbon's canoe drifted out of the bay.

Big Ocean was glad Little Gibbon had made it through the Fog Covered Shipping Lanes. She was glad he had avoided the Giant Drink Of Saltwater and had drifted out of the Bay Of Sharks With Big Teeth. But now he was in quite a bit of danger. Little Gibbon was headed towards the Strong Current To Open Ocean.

Big Ocean sent some waves to peek into Little Gibbon's canoe.

"He has no paddle," the first wave said.

"He has no water," the second wave said.

"He has no food," the third wave said.

"He has no life jacket," the fourth wave said.

The waves were making Little Gibbon a little seasick.

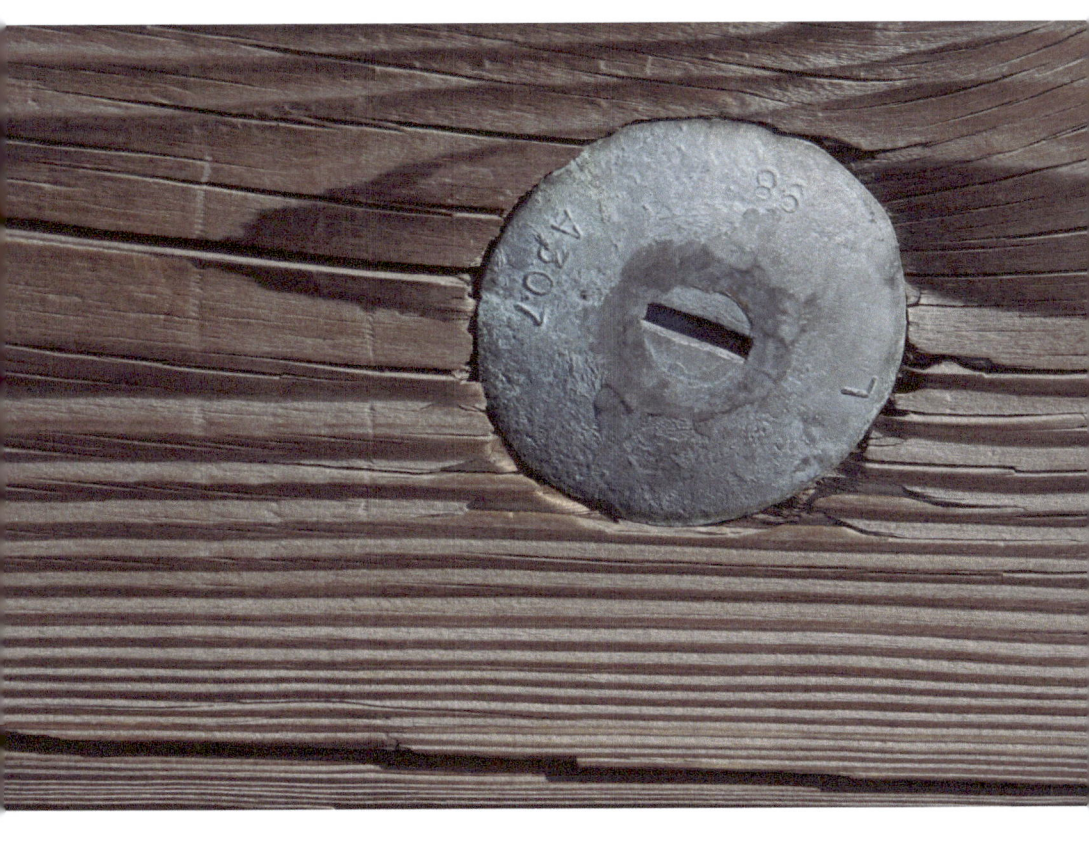

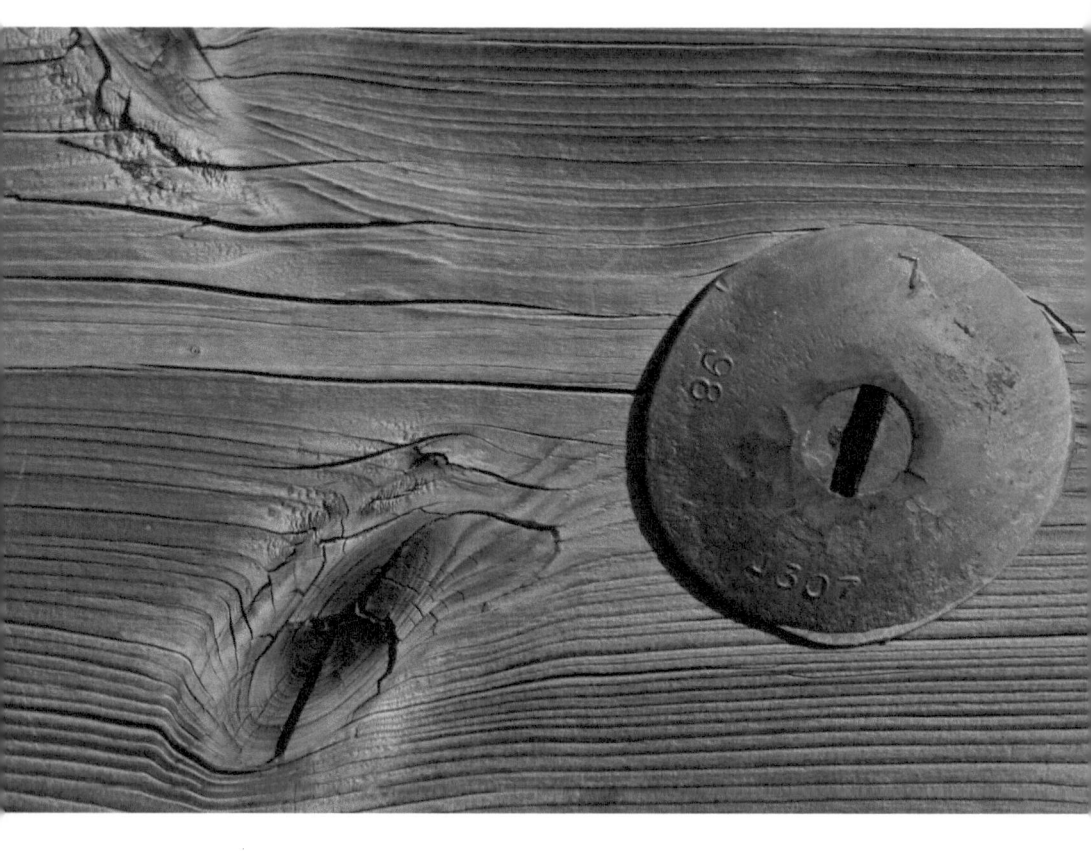

Big Ocean frowned. Once Little Gibbon got caught in the Strong Current, the nearest land would be 5,000 miles away. It would be a long trip without food, water or a paddle.

"Big Wind," said Big Ocean, "See that canoe? My currents are taking it out to sea. Could you blow Little Gibbon back to land instead?"

Big Wind laughed.

"You know I can't do favors for every foolish person who goes out on the water. You're *covered* with ships, and they all want something different. Today Little Gibbon is lucky, because today I feel like blowing towards shore. But if Little Gibbon counts on me for a favor tomorrow, he'll be in for an adventure."

"He might like an adventure tomorrow," said Big Ocean. "But today I think he'd rather be back on shore."

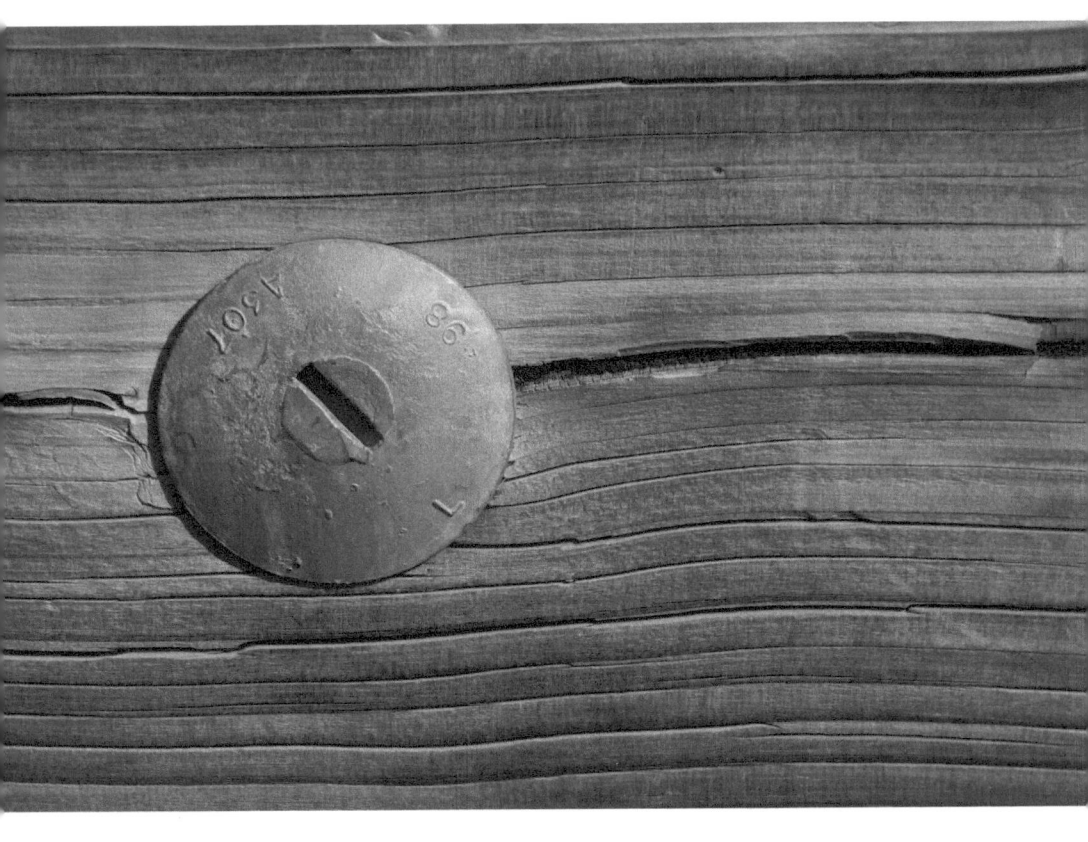

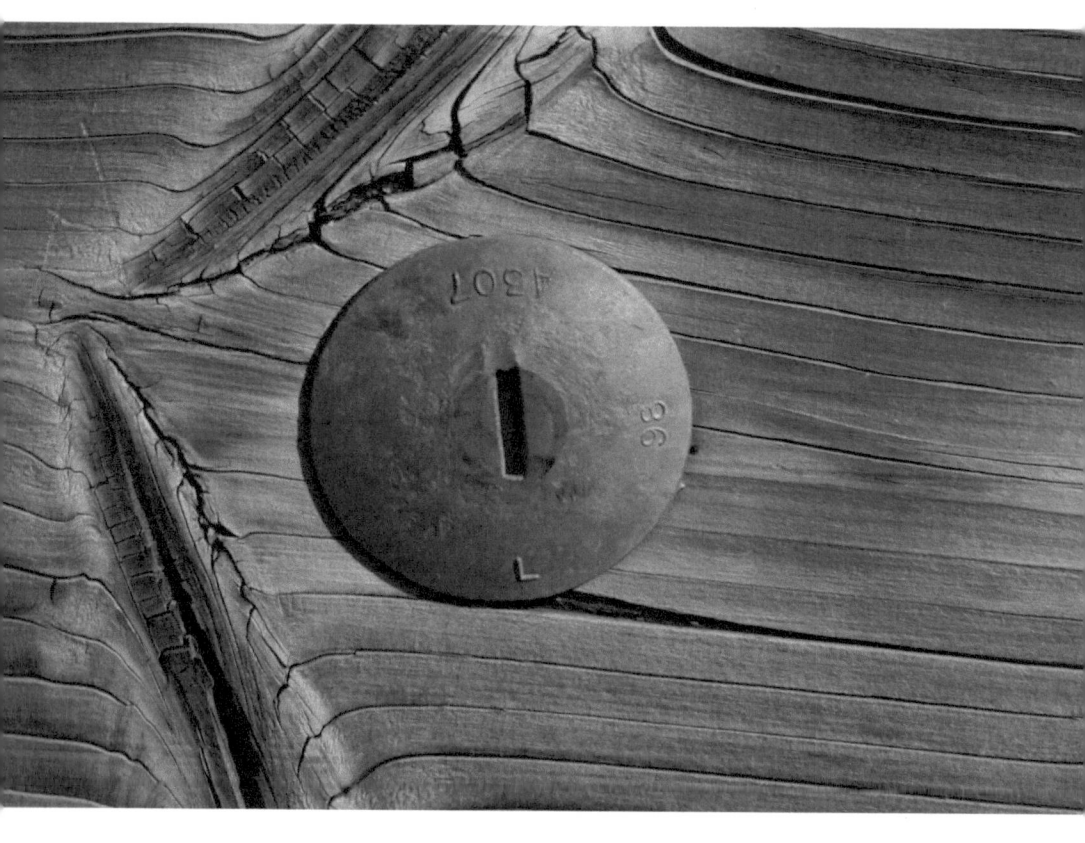

Big Wind started to blow. And blow. And blow. The whitecaps increased and the waves got more choppy. Soon what had been a pleasant ride was quite rough.

Little Gibbon was ready to ask Big Wind to stop, but then he noticed he was getting closer to shore, even though Big Ocean's current was heading out to sea. Soon after that he fell asleep. He didn't mean to, but he did. It was his time for a nap.

Big Ocean thought Little Gibbon had had enough adventures for one day, so she didn't wake him when his canoe passed the Waters Smashing Against Lighthouse Rock.

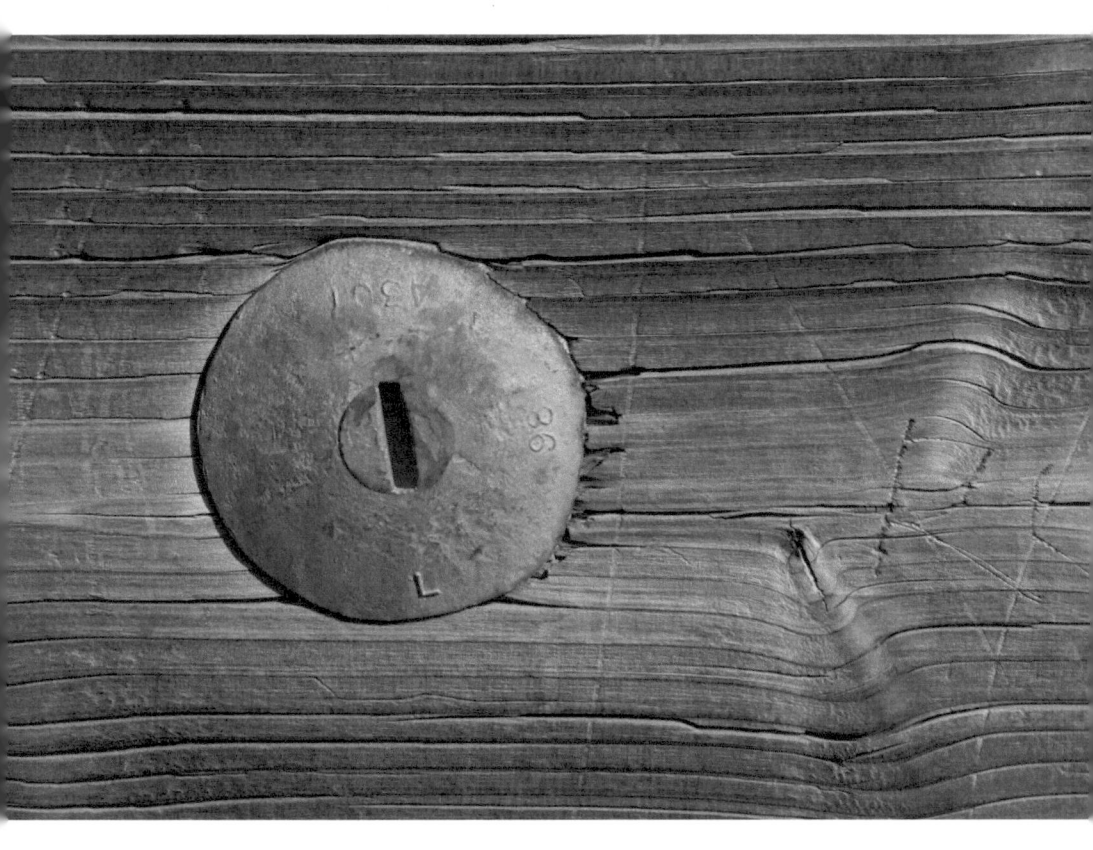

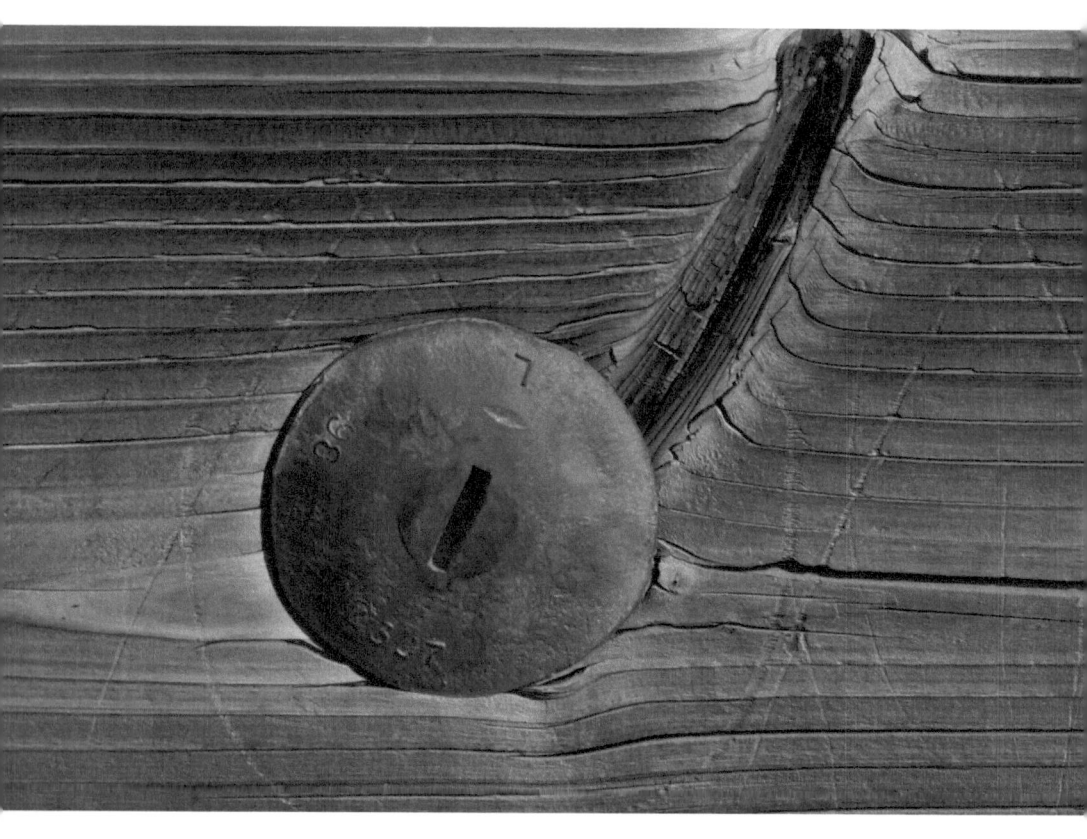

Big Ocean didn't wake Little Gibbon when his canoe went through the Surf With Stinging Jellyfish.

Big Ocean didn't wake Little Gibbon when his canoe got a big push onto dry land from the Massive Rogue Wave.

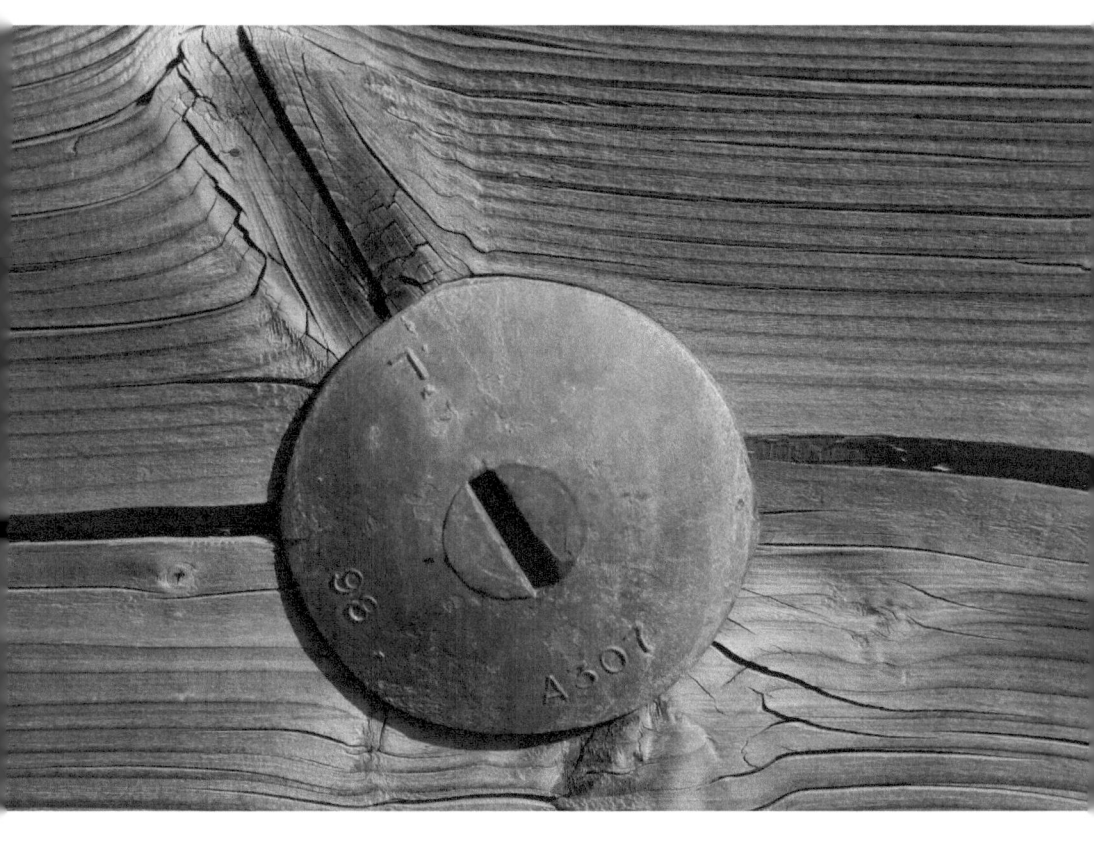

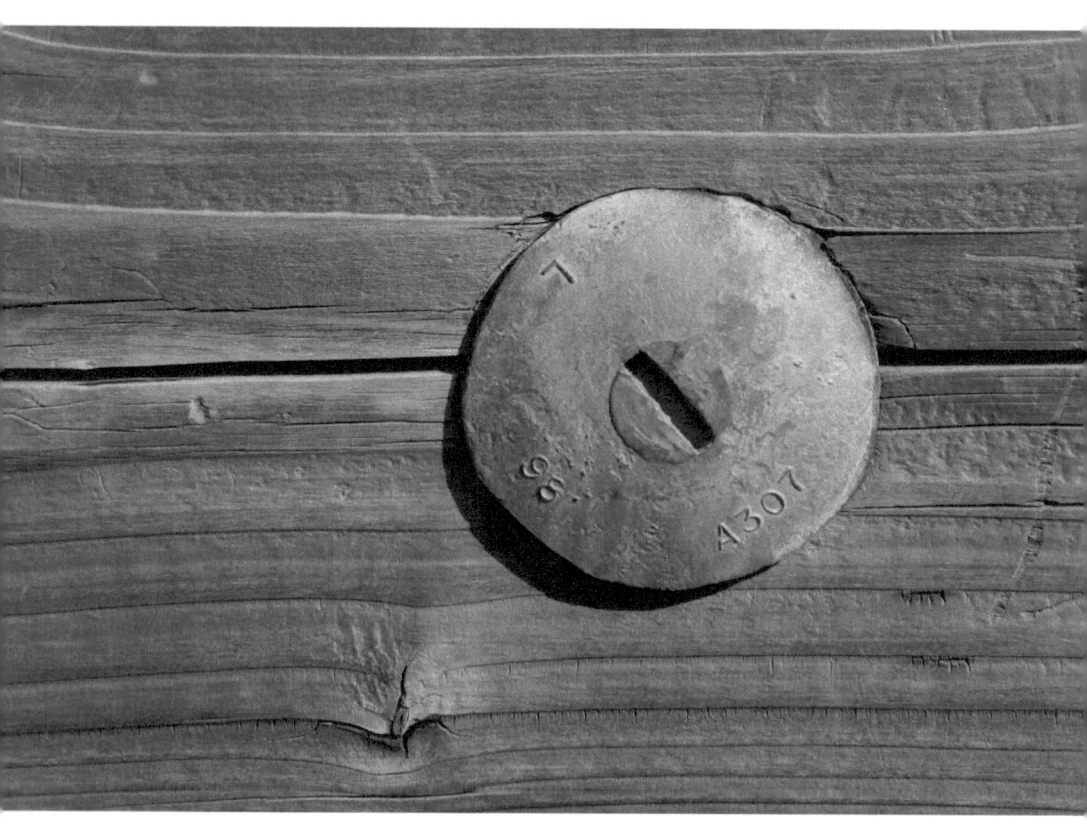

Big Moon helped Big Ocean retreat a bit so Little Gibbon would be on dry ground when he woke up.

Little Gibbon had had enough adventures for one day, thought Big Ocean. There was always tomorrow.

~~

Reflection questions

When have you forgotten to bring something that you really needed?

Of all the adventures you have had so far, which ones were best?

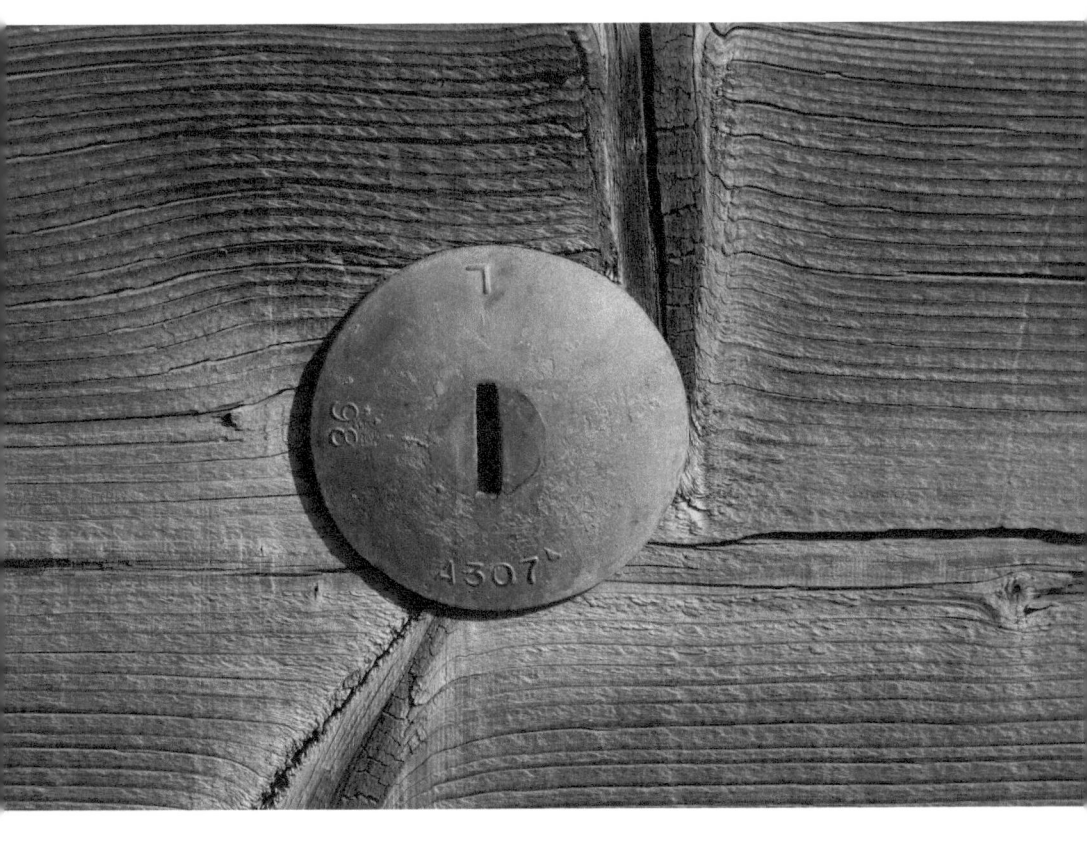

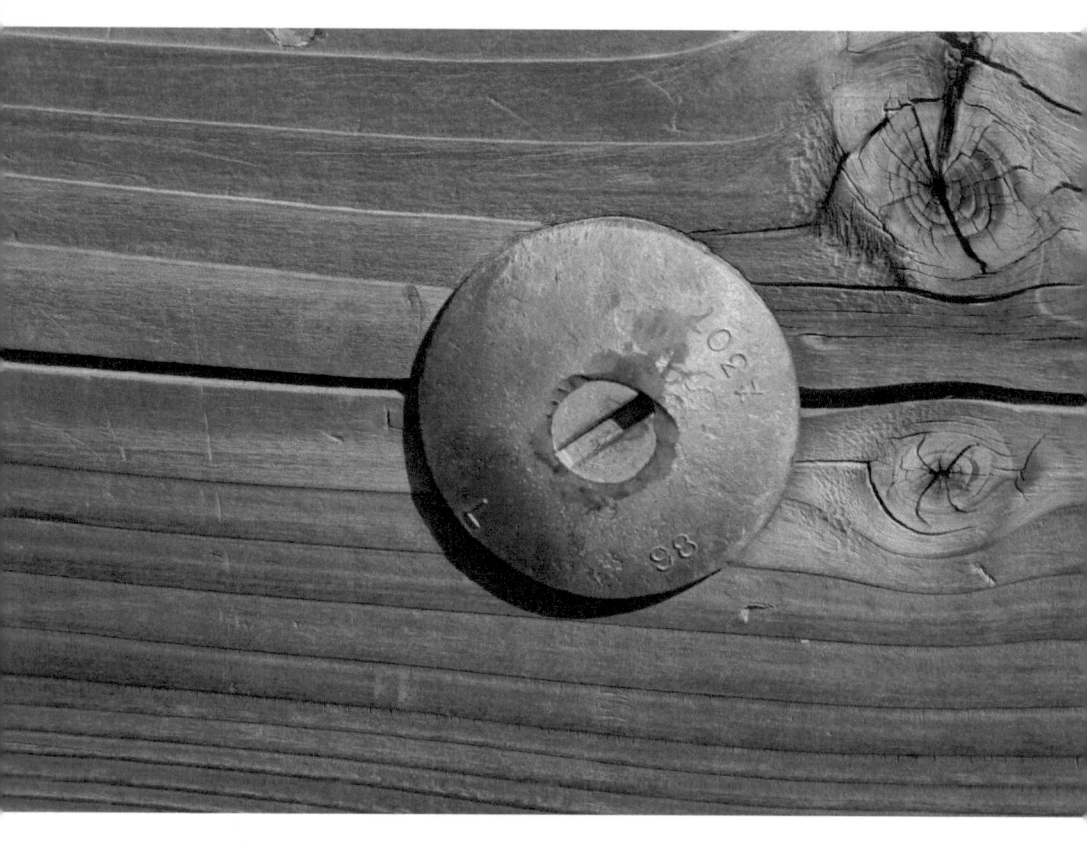

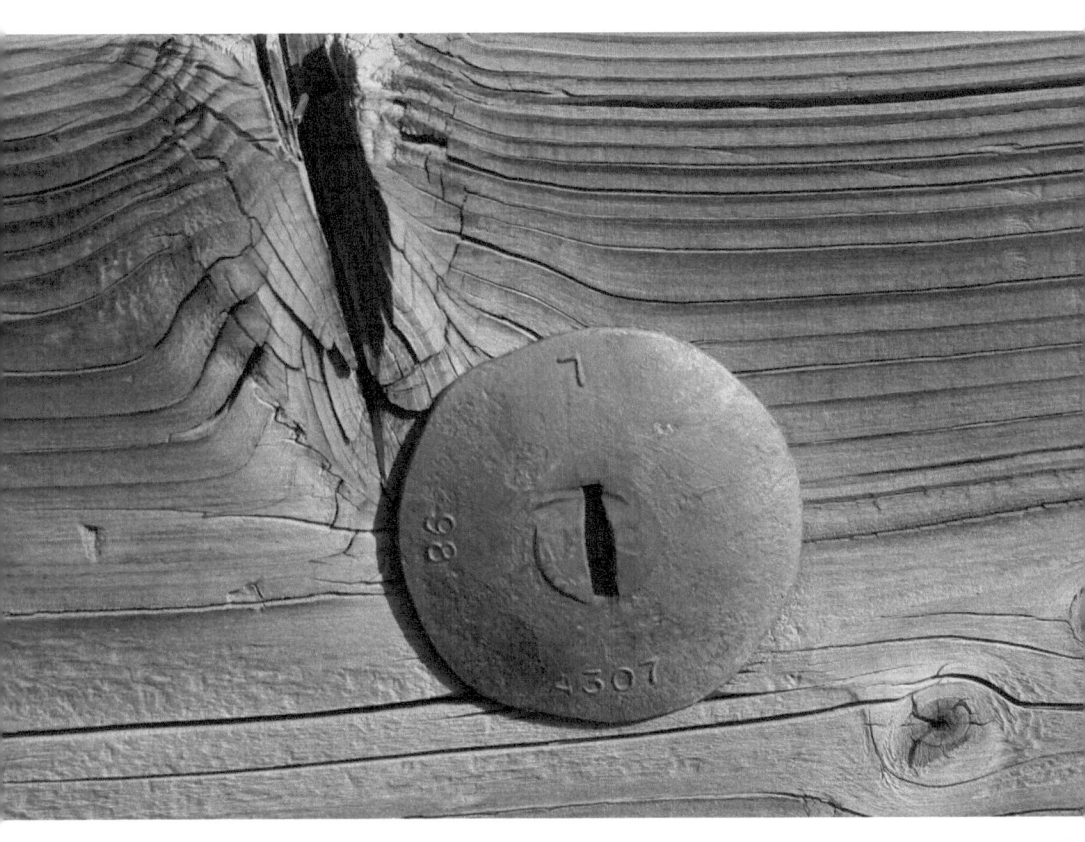

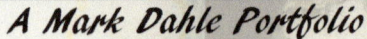

A Mark Dahle Portfolio

Monkey Brains On Big Mountain

Little Gibbon's Big Adventures #3

This Mark Dahle Portfolio includes a photo of a colorful abstract painting, twenty-six outstanding photographs from Spokane and Eastern Washington, and a story about a gibbon who liked adventures.

On Big Mountain the weather could change in less than an hour, but at the moment things couldn't be nicer. There was very little danger, unless Little Gibbon got lost.

The path Little Gibbon was on headed straight to the Confusing Intersection Of Many Trails.

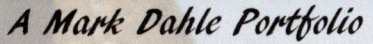

A Mark Dahle Portfolio

Farmer Jane

This Mark Dahle Portfolio includes a beautiful painting, twenty-five gorgeous photographs from the Netherlands, and a story about Farmer Jane.

Jane didn't know that farmers have troubles.

But she was about to discover how *many* troubles they have.

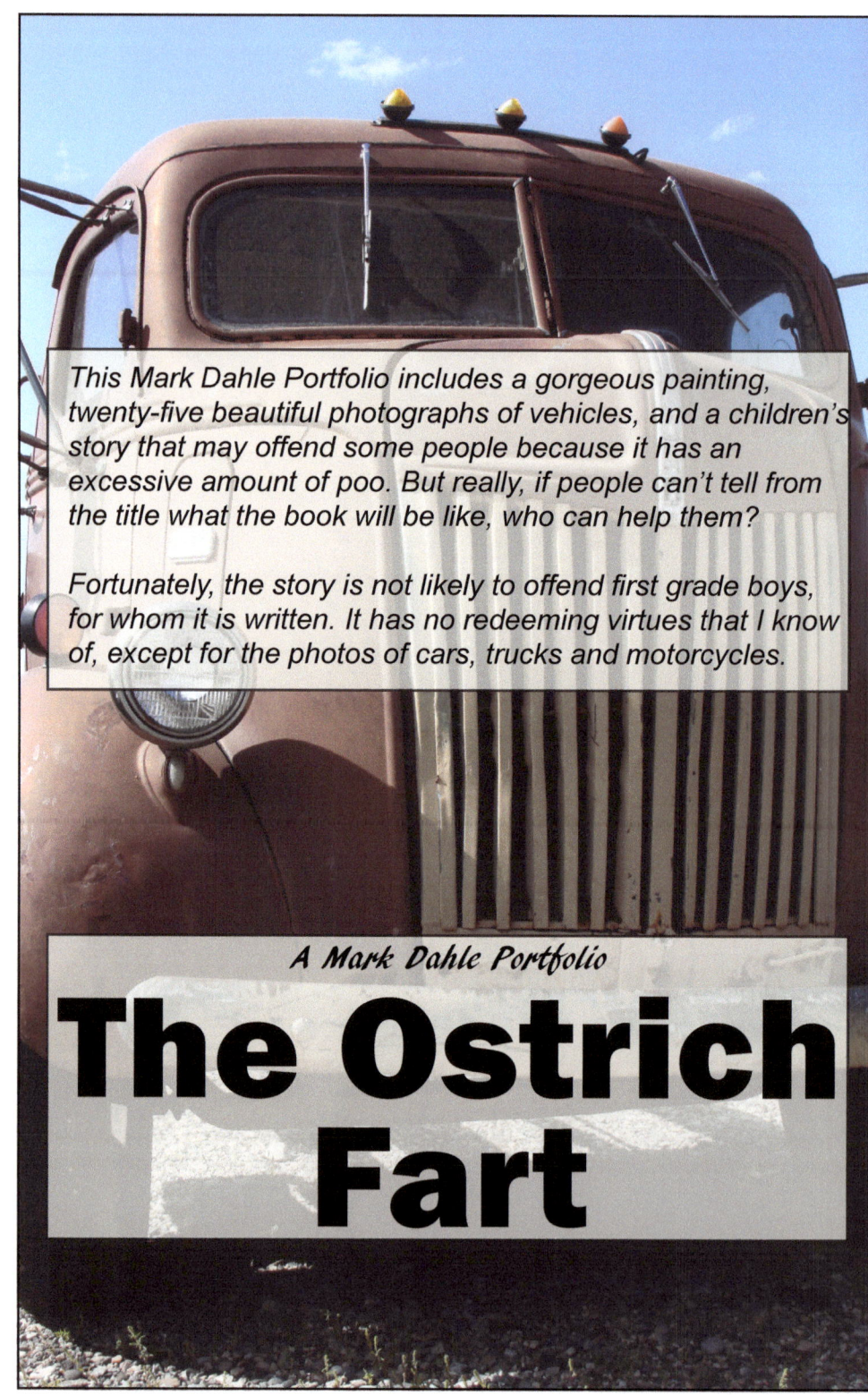

This Mark Dahle Portfolio includes a gorgeous painting, twenty-five beautiful photographs of vehicles, and a children's story that may offend some people because it has an excessive amount of poo. But really, if people can't tell from the title what the book will be like, who can help them?

Fortunately, the story is not likely to offend first grade boys, for whom it is written. It has no redeeming virtues that I know of, except for the photos of cars, trucks and motorcycles.

A Mark Dahle Portfolio

The Ostrich Fart

www.ingramcontent.com/pod-product-compliance
Lightning Source LLC
Chambersburg PA
CBHW040856180526
45159CB00001B/435